ANEW

ANEW

Prayer Journey, Guide, and Journal Companion

A guide of prayers and practices to help break free of psychological challenges

Danielle Presume

CONTENTS

anew: a · new

/əˈn(y)oo͞/

adverb LITERARY

1. in a new or different and typically more positive way.
2. once more; again.
   "tears filled her eyes anew"

Synonyms: again, once more, once again, a second time, afresh

"Definition of anew in English," www.lexico.com, Oxford University Press, Lexico.com, LLC, May 13, 2019, https://www.lexico.com/en/definition/anew.

PREFACE

Mental illness. A term that I never thought would, could, or should apply to me.

I had my first anxiety attack in 2010, the first red flag for me that my life had been changing. Panic and extreme anxiety and a cloud of darkness became my new normal. I was twenty-four and in the midst of a deep and dark battle.

I knew the names of the feelings and thoughts I had. But, at the time, I didn't know what triggered them or how to get help other than through prescription medication. Within a year, I had been diagnosed with severe anxiety disorder. As more years passed, I was diagnosed with social anxiety disorder, depression, and even PTSD (post-traumatic stress disorder).

Eventually I learned it was all triggered by trauma. Trauma that I thought was normal. I was in an environment rooted in a relationship that tore me down verbally, mentally, and emotionally. My normal looked normal on the outside but was unhealthy and toxic. I stayed in this environment for nine years before making the decision to leave. I realize now that was the best decision I could've made for everyone involved. Leaving, though, was just the beginning. I had to reprogram my mind and find a healthy balance emotionally to unlearn all of the unhealthy habits and thought patterns I had developed.

Prior to leaving, I had finally realized that the cycles of panic, depression, and pain were not normal or healthy. Everything was getting worse; I was getting worse. I started to notice how the patterns of intrusive and troubling thoughts, compulsive mannerisms, extreme fear, and increased social awkwardness coincided with the weekly and sometimes daily stresses and triggers I was facing. The symptoms had become my personality.

My toxic homelife had become familiar, and I didn't realize how unhealthy it really was. And it had a name: abuse. It was not so much what someone was doing to me than it was what I had allowed to happen to myself. It wasn't until I opened up about what I was experiencing, in desperation with someone I trusted, that my journey of healing truly began. I was in denial regarding the truth of just how bad things were for me. I had to dig . . . deep. I had to look at how this began and how it managed to continue for so many years, gradually altering my mental health and pulling me further away from who I was created to be: aware, bold, fearless.

My environment went from carefree and light to burdened and heavy. My surroundings gradually contributed to my mental demise. I was fighting and didn't know how to fight. I had become only a shadow of my true self. I was tired. I tried to escape through church, projects, business — anything. All of this to get away from the looming darkness that stole my breath away. I couldn't focus. Once the anxiety came, a pit of darkness wasn't far behind, and I would lose interest, hope, and any motivation I had. I was struggling. I felt like a failure.

And then came the big question. The major concern. I often thought to myself, how could someone who claims to be a Christian live like this? Running from darkness? Struggling to truly be happy and free? I realize that there are many other Christians who have had these same questions and who have suffered in silence. I know now that my struggles and imperfections do not disqualify me from being a Christian. I spent years learning prayers and scriptures that no doubt helped me get through the dark times I faced and even set me up for my current growth and healing. But I wanted to overcome it. I was coping, but I needed to be consistent, strategic, systematic, and intentional to truly see a positive change in my quality of life. I believed that consistently, strategically, and intentionally living my life in a way that supported my psychological healing, growth, and development would yield success. So in January 2019, I decided to take steps to change my life for the better. I left the familiar yet toxic life I was living and took the unfamiliar road of learning about mental and emotional health. I reacquainted myself with God from a healthy mental and emotional space. It was painful and uncomfortable, but oh so worth it. I can honestly say that with persistence in prayer, therapy, hard work, and plenty of "mental health days," I have begun to live and enjoy my life in ways I could not have even imagined. And that's what I want to help you do in this book.

It didn't feel like it was better at first. I had to leave places and people I knew were not good for my mental, emotional, and physical health. It was hard. But I kept seeking God's guidance as best as I could. Although I sought God before, I realized that I had to make a change in my mindset and lifestyle before I could really get the healing I was looking for. Little did I know that the toughest year of my life would turn out to be the most fruitful.

Anew is a true testament to how God can transform us if we let him. *Anew* is the triumphant culmination of every dark day I faced as I battled depression, anxiety, and trauma day after day. This guide holds every strategic tool, big and small, that got me from the "weeping that endured for the night" to "joy that comes in the morning."

So how did *Anew: Prayer Guide and Journey* come to be?

Long story short, I cried out to God like never before. I made up my mind I would follow that cry by answering an altar call at church the following Sunday. At the altar call, my pastor told me that I should write a prayer journal to help others break free from mental illness. I was the one asking for help, so I didn't know what use God might have for a book from me, but I felt a calling, and I chased it. I wanted to be free. I wanted to please and obey God. I wanted to help others.

What I understand now is that God knows his children. He created us. He knows me and what he created me for and what I am capable of. So when I felt God wanted me to write a book while I went through my healing, I decided to write it. Although I can't say I was fully persuaded at first, I can say in the end I clearly see how I was able to get the breakthrough I cried out for.

I thank God for the help that he sent me and the help he led me to. I thank God for the unwavering love and support of my mother, Gwendolyn Rozier-Leonard. I thank God for wise counsel in my pastors Apostle Antonio Williams and Prophetess Angel Williams. I thank God for the words my father, Ronald Leonard, spoke to me as a child that I am seeing manifest now. I thank God for my tribe of friends and family who always seemed to say the right thing that kept me moving forward. I thank God for my therapist, Vianca, and the work she has done with me. Now I know more than ever that all things work together for my good because I love him!

Before starting the work outlined in the following chapters, if I haven't made it clear already, understand that this prayer journey will take some tenacity on your part. I'm assuming you have this book because you fight battles (to some degree) in your mind. Anything from indecisiveness and confusion to chronic anxiety, depression, and PTSD. All of those can be remedied by applying the principles I have outlined in this journal.

By no means is this book a cure, extensive, nor should it be the only tool in your toolbox. This book is a supplement that says there is a way out and you are not alone. I want to shine more light on mental health. The only way to fix something is to acknowledge its existence. Pretending that it's not there or just not a big deal will not heal anyone, nor will it help to depend solely on medication that is meant to help your symptoms. So while I am happy that you decided to allow me to be part of your journey, I encourage you to invite others along to assist and support you. Find a therapist, seek wise spiritual counsel, get out of unhealthy relationships and environments, get in tune with yourself, and most importantly get connected to God through scripture and prayer. *Prayer*. Prayer is not something in and of itself—it is part of a whole. It is the middleman between problem and solution. Prayer is the bridge that makes change accessible.

Although this is a prayer journal, think of this as a prayer journey with paved and unpaved roads that your prayer will repair and replace to help your walk become smoother. Faith without works is dead (James 2:26). Your legwork and your prayers will go hand in hand to get you to your new day. "Life and death lie in the power of your tongue" (Prov. 18:21).

INTRODUCTION

MY MENTAL AND EMOTIONAL BREAKTHROUGH

It has been about nine years since my first anxiety attack and subsequent diagnosis of severe anxiety disorder. As I look back over my battles, I realize that by the time I recognized the triggers, it was too late. I had suffered for years before I fully understood how stress, my environment, and my relationships could make or break my healing process (or lack thereof). The blessing in all of that is I can now share from experience how I coped and how my breakthrough has finally begun to manifest. I learned how to address not only internal issues but also the stressors and factors that contributed to my mental and emotional makeup. My spiritual health and beliefs were also affected. The way that I looked at my relationships became flawed because I was looking through a lens cracked by anxiety and fear. I felt misunderstood, rejected, and unwanted, loving God but not loving myself. I heard *anointed*, *talented*, *creative*, and *gifted* from others and only believed the words when they said them. I struggled to believe in myself and only went forward because I wanted to please God. I wanted people to believe God existed and was all-powerful. But I didn't believe in myself, so my attempts to showcase God went only so far because in my mind I could only do so much, and the value of my efforts seemed minimal.

Even amid all that darkness, I knew God. Even when I allowed myself to be disrespected and mistreated, I knew God. My approach was not always perfect. I put myself into settings that were foreign to me just so I could get to know God.

My trials caused me to run to God in ways I am not sure I would have otherwise. I suffered, I struggled, I fought, and sometimes I feel I failed. Spiritually, though, I grew. I thought, how could it be that my spiritual walk seems to elevate, yet my mental and emotional health are so out of whack? But while on a walk with friends, I was reminded that all these things work together for my good and that at the end of the day, my trials will be able to help someone else. Maybe you won't have to suffer as I did for as long as I did. Maybe you will recover more quickly from reading this and writing your own entries. Maybe these words and scriptures will comfort you and cause you to realize you are not alone.

Trust that God has a perfect plan for your life and will see you through it all. I hope to inspire you to be truthful and seek truth for yourself about where you are, how you got there, and what you need to escape that place. As you go into the next segment of this book, I pray you receive every word in love and that you are blessed and inspired to push until you get your breakthrough and your new day! There is some space in the back of this book for you to journal as you journey in prayer and practice. Of course, you can get a notebook for journaling as well. Either way, I highly encourage you to engage with each chapter and reflect on what touches you and how.

GOING DEEPER: INTRUSIVE THOUGHTS

Intrusive thoughts have been one of my greatest pitfalls over the years. Intrusive thoughts are distressing thoughts. In hindsight, I realized these thoughts played on things I honored and valued by causing me to think of them in a negative and sometimes inappropriate light, which brought more distress and anxiety. The intrusive thoughts would occur so often that my brain would anticipate them then fixate on the thought. For me these thoughts would be against God, church, and even people I loved and looked up to. After a bout (days, possibly weeks), I panicked.

I really hoped God would send a word to reassure me. And what he sent was his Word.

One morning after a near meltdown, he made it so that the scripture of the day was 2 Corinthians 10:5:

> We demolish arguments and every pretension that sets itself up against the knowledge of God, and we take captive every thought to make it obedient to Christ.

This scripture reminded me of the power I have to conquer what could possibly destroy me. It reminded me that God hears me, and he's always with me because he sent me help when I needed it.

You have that same power. Do not allow unwanted

thoughts to be a burden that you just accept as part of yourself. Do not become familiar with them. Mental health is a stigma that not many discuss openly, especially when it comes to unwanted, uncontrollable thoughts. When I first began having these thoughts—naturally because I feared I had angered God—I became extremely anxious. Later, I realized that my intrusive thoughts always coincided with moments of high stress and anxiety. I recognized what my triggers were and that these thoughts were normally centered around specific events, themes, or thoughts. The focus of the thoughts never really changed over the years, either. In fact, it became a fixation, where once the thought came, I worried so much about it that I would almost always anticipate the thought when I saw or heard a particular trigger. If this is you, I encourage you to seek spiritual advisement and clinical therapy and treatment.

Before I realized the effect that trauma played on my mental health, I believed that I only needed deliverance from evil spirits.

The more I learned about deliverance and the more I learned about mental health, I understood that not everything dealing with mental health has to do with an exorcism. Satan can worm into our thoughts especially if he sees that it will paralyze you with fear as it did me. But the good news is, you have the ultimate power.

You may need to change your surroundings, cut certain people off, or repent of a bad habit or sinful lifestyle. Either way, bondage is bondage, and Jesus set us free from it all. As long as you truly love God and desire to live a pure, holy, and righteous life in Christ, God will heal you and deliver you. But be honest and transparent with him and with yourself.

Even by completing this journal, you are doing the legwork

to get to your freedom. Continue to do what you can and watch as God does the rest.

When I feel as if thoughts and worries are caving in on me, I pray, worship, and speak God's Word over myself. I speak affirmations, and I take back my authority and my mind. I also recognize the need to cater to my mental health by resting, avoiding stress, and partaking in fulfilling and meaningful hobbies and events. Do what makes you happy and brings you joy. Fill your days with delighting in God! Trust him with your time, energy, and faith.

NO SELF-PITY

You may have been mistreated, betrayed, or even left for dead. You may have been neglected, abandoned, cheated on, talked about, or lied to. There is no doubt that everyday injustices occur to people around the world. There is no doubt that trauma took place in your life and caused the way you think, speak, and feel to be jaded. But one thing I have found to be true is that self-pity and victimization are of no benefit to the mind.

You have read about not wallowing in your sadness—that is what self-pity is. You must prevent what happened to you from navigating your personality and your outlook. It took me years to realize that I allowed myself to be a twenty-four-hours-a-day, seven-days-a-week victim. Yes, unfair things were said and done to me. Yes, I experienced heartbreak and pain. But I was so used to fighting those emotions that it seeped out of my pores at times. I wanted everyone to understand my pain and even hoped someone would fix it. But I had to realize that not everyone is going to understand—not everyone is going to help or even care. So then what? Will I just remain stuck, or will I get up and choose to stop being the victim?

I sought a therapist. I talked about what was really going on in my home and in my head. I chose to leave unhealthy situations and habits. I chose to stop being the victim and start believing that I am the victor. *My life will be abundant and full of joy.* I chose to walk that truth out.

Just like getting up after sitting on your legs for a long time, the first few steps are painful and uncomfortable. You might not be able to feel your legs, but God already taught you how to walk so you know what to do. Do it no matter what you feel like. Do it no matter what tries to stop you or get in your way. Do not let anyone or anything get in your way. Banish self-pity.

Now speak life!

YOUR FOUNDATION

Therefore everyone who hears these words of mine and puts them into practice is like a wise man who built his house on the rock.

Matthew 7:24

When confusion, fear, and paranoia cause you to believe one thing and doubt the next, it's okay to stop and put things into perspective, but it is also good to check your foundation. Is it God, or is it you, or is it people, or is it your will and vain and crazy imagination? If it isn't God, put everything else down. Ask God to help you make him your foundation. Ask him to help you to hear and know his voice. Ask him to help you quiet all other voices, to sharpen your discernment, and to refresh your mind with peace and understanding. Others are here to help but will never take God's place.

Make sure your walk is all God, including your intentions. You may mean well, but make sure you are living your life to honor God and not to act the way people think of you outside of God. You can honor God by honoring the people he has placed in your life, but be careful not to make them idols or cause you to lose focus on God.

God is your foundation. You aren't, nor are your friends, so start strong and build tall.

Prayer

Father, thank you for your unfailing love, mercy and grace. I acknowledge that I haven't always allowed you to be the foundation of my life and life's decisions. I recognize the value and necessity of having a solid foundation and ask that you help me to have that foundation in you. Show me areas of my life that are on shaky ground and help me to replace that shaky ground with your immovable ground. Father, I welcome you to restructure the foundation of my heart and my mind so that I will not be easily swayed or moved by others but grounded in you. I thank you and give you praise now for the transformation that is to come and that is happening even now. In Jesus' name, Amen.

Focus

Who or what is your foundation? How and why did they become your foundation?

What can you do to transition to God being your foundation?

Scripture

"Come near to God and he will come near to you. Wash your hands, you sinners, and purify your hearts, you double-minded" (James 4:8).

"Therefore everyone who hears these words of mine and puts them into practice is like a wise man who built his house on the rock. The rain came down, the streams rose, and the winds blew and beat against that house; yet it did not fall, because it had its foundation on the rock. But everyone who hears these words of mine and does not put them into practice is like a foolish man who built his house on sand. The rain came down, the streams rose, and the winds blew and beat against that house, and it fell with a great crash" (Matt. 7:24-27)

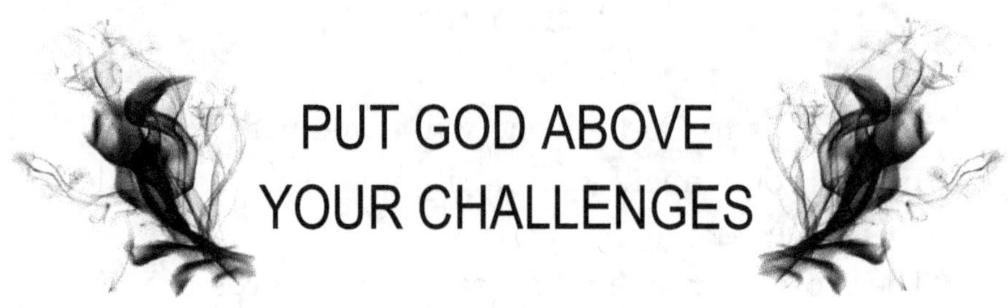

PUT GOD ABOVE YOUR CHALLENGES

So do not worry, saying, 'What shall we eat?' or 'What shall we drink?' or 'What shall we wear?' For the pagans run after all these things, and your heavenly Father knows that you need them. But seek first his kingdom and his righteousness, and all these things will be given to you as well.

Matthew 6:31-33

Your things are in the way. Yes, your things: worry, work, anxiety, regret, fear, family, possessions, money. All of these are significant to some degree, but they all have a place. Whatever you have going on, God should take precedence over it all. God is the one who provides. But it's easy to forget that when our possessions make us feel either self-sufficient or lacking, it can be very easy to depend on them to make us feel better, to resolve that problem instead of figuring out why it's a problem in the first place.

God wants your heart and your mind by being the influence of your daily decisions, big and small. I challenge you to evaluate what is currently occupying your mind and your time. Is God (and his guiding precepts) at the forefront? If not, then what or who is? Putting God first is not neglecting your responsibilities nor is it disregarding your hobbies or interests. Putting God first helped me to keep from getting carried away with any one thing and to keep my day-to-day living healthy and balanced.

What's going to happen to me if I can't get it together? What if I don't succeed when I follow my dreams? How will I get the money to eat, get to work, and pay these legal fees? These are some thoughts that I allowed to circulate in my mind over and over. Leaving little to no room in my mind for God. Most if not all of those anxiety-inducing thoughts were all questions to nobody. I even worried, excessively and obsessively, about displeasing God. But I did all that worrying and wondering without even acknowledging him or talking to him about it. The cause of my worry was getting in the way of the connection to the one who had the solutions. He advises us to "acknowledge Him in all of our ways and He will direct our paths (Proverbs 3:6)". Your busy life and mind may be interfering with the best relationship and guidance you could ever have.

Sometimes you literally have to stop everything, be still, and seek God. No matter how pressing the issue may be. Once I began to seek God more in the midst of those pressing issues and, instead of worrying, I spent time with him, my faith increased. I recognized that the value of our relationship outweighed the value of the things I had allowed to get in his position in my mind and heart. In other words, when I focused my thoughts on God's promises, it left little room for anything else to take over my mind. His Word negates and refutes every worry you could ever have through faith and through practical application. Instead of allowing my circumstances to overwhelm me, I would stop everything, and I would find a way to connect with God. I would literally seek him in praise, prayer, and scripture until I felt peace. I recognized the powerful and positive shifts that happened to me mentally and emotionally when I truly put everything else aside and made him the center of my will. Since I am a visual person, I would literally imagine myself putting my anxious thoughts and feelings in a basket and handing them over to God.

Making God your treasure is only the first step. Even treasure can be buried and lost due to neglect. The task is in keeping God as your treasure when other things try to come in and take that position. In Matthew 6:21, Jesus puts it like this: "For where your treasure is, there your heart will be also." By keeping him as your treasure you are allowing God to be in your heart. You are allowing him to be the source of your life and your strength. You are creating a safe place in which to dwell with him constantly. He won't only be an oasis in the dry, desolate deserts of life, but he will be a constant stronghold for a lifestyle of peace, serenity, and spiritual wealth.

God can be trusted not only to hold your most valuable possessions but to exchange them for something far more valuable: his presence. I realized that although God is surely always present and mindful of me, I can sometimes take him for granted. I also realized that I add value to my life by actively enjoying the treasure of his presence.

As the heart is to your body, visualize God being the same to your mental, emotional, and spiritual health. We cannot see the heart, but we know it is there and we get up every day expecting it to work without a second thought. I learned that I thrive most when I nurture my relationship with God just like most humans thrive physically when they exercise and eat right.

Prayer

Father, you are the most high God! God of the heavens and of all the earth. I lift you today in my mind, my heart, and my life. Every day as you mold me, I pray that I will get to know more and more about you so my faith and trust in you will increase. I pray that in all my ways, I will acknowledge you, and that this will cause you to direct my path. I pray my trust in you grows over my circumstances and possessions. I pray that I won't take the treasure of your presence and your love for granted. I welcome you to continue to show me ways I can glorify you and deny myself and anyone or anything that may try to replace you in my life. In Jesus's name, amen.

Focus

Consider how God has impacted your life and how your life would be different without him.

Scripture

"You make known to me the path of life; you will fill me with joy in your presence, with eternal pleasures at your right hand" (Ps. 16:11).

"For where your treasure is, there your heart will be also" (Matt. 6:21).

CHOOSE NOT TO WORRY— CHOOSE NOT TO FEAR

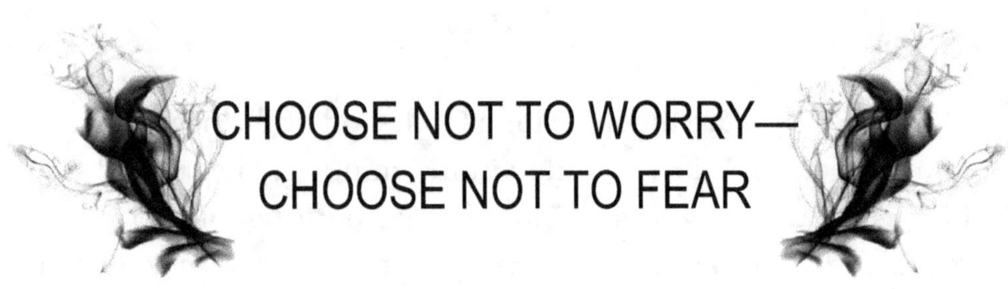

Cast all your anxiety on him because he cares for you.
1 Peter 5:7

Fear and worry are natural reactions to situations in our lives, but remember that you always have a choice as to how you can react. Ultimately, your choice is between faith and doubt. You either choose to trust that God will work it out—or not. Many times, we worry about something that God has already worked out, and we fear an outcome we can't see.

Facing your fear is the best way to build your faith. Trusting God and not what you see, hear, and feel is the ultimate goal. It is not always easy to trust God first, but it is necessary for your peace. It will take practice, persistence, and patience. Most importantly it will take faith.

I am writing this from my current and past experiences, but this biblical principle has stood the test of time:

> Do not be anxious about anything, but in every situation, by prayer and petition, with thanksgiving, present your requests to God. And the peace of God, which transcends all

understanding, will guard your hearts and your minds in Christ Jesus (Phil. 4:6-7).

This scripture tells us what our choices are and the benefits of choosing God. So try it! Pray — tell God what you need, thank him, and experience his peace and joy. Several times, I allowed fear to creep back in despite my prayer. If that happens to you, it's okay. Just repeat the same formula. With God, you will win. Persevere.

Prayer

Father God, I thank you for freedom. I thank you that I do not have to live in bondage to fear. I thank you that your perfect love is working in me and casting out all fear. I welcome you into my heart today and welcome your peace, which surpasses all understanding. In Jesus's name, amen.

Focus

Give God your worries and fears by talking to him about them and then spending time with him through prayer, worship, or Bible study. I like "walk and talks" to escape from my worries to be with God.

Practice replacing negative and fearful thoughts with positive ones for the renewal of your mind.

Scripture

"Cast your cares on the LORD and he will sustain you; he will never let the righteous be shaken" (Ps. 55:22).

"Do not be anxious about anything, but in every situation, by prayer and petition, with thanksgiving, present your requests to God. And the peace of God, which transcends all understanding, will guard your hearts and your minds in Christ Jesus" (Phil. 4:6-7).

DON'T FORGET TO BREATHE

> *Then the LORD God formed a man from the dust of the ground and breathed into his nostrils the breath of life, and the man became a living being.*
>
> Genesis 2:7

Sometimes we build our own walls of Jericho. Each worry is a brick that we stack until we can't see God, our eyes only on the worries we've amassed. Sometimes I catch myself one hundred bricks into building that wall before I realize I'm not even breathing, literally. My mind runs one hundred miles a minute, each possible problem as prominent as the last. Heart palpitations. Panic. Shortness of breath.

You may recognize these as symptoms of anxiety. Although diagnosed with a disorder that justified these symptoms, I did not want them to be my norm. I knew that something could and should be done to change this.

Even after pinpointing the causes of my anxiety, the symptoms did not change. My brain already knew how to feel the way it did. So I had to learn how to reprogram my brain and body to relax.

I had to make changes. Rest, thought consciousness and

meditation, and breathing exercises. I share breathing techniques below that I use regularly. Your breath is a blessing. Cherish it, and let it heal you.

Prayer

Father, thank you for the first gift you gave to man — breath. Help me to train my mind to remember you when worry begins to set in. Help me to tap into your peace daily and live a life of serenity, even when there is chaos all around me. Make me to lie down in green pastures and walk beside the still waters. I want to experience the beauty of your peace, and I ask that you help me to identify the people, situations, and things that take my eyes off you and that can cause a wall to mount between us. Take away the precedence these things have over my health. Draw me close today, Father, as I release all worry and choose breath and life! In Jesus's name, amen.

Focus

Take time throughout the day to breathe and get oxygen to your brain and body.

Focus on the changes you notice after the breathing exercises.

Scripture

"Let everything that has breath praise the LORD. Praise the LORD" (Ps. 150:6).

"The Spirit of God has made me, and the breath of the Almighty gives me life" (Job 33:4).

Breathing exercises

Exercise 1.

Breathe in deeply and slowly through your nose while counting to four. Be careful to breathe in so your diaphragm rises, not your chest. Hold that breath for four counts and then release slowly out of your mouth for four counts. Repeat this ten times in one sitting and repeat throughout the day as needed.

Exercise 2.

Press down on your right nostril with your index finger. Breathe in slowly through your left nostril while counting to four. Hold that breath for four counts. Press down on your left nostril and release that breath out of the right nostril over four counts. Still holding down your left nostril, breathe in through the right nostril and repeat this pattern.

GOD'S WORD >
MY EMOTIONS

The mind governed by the flesh is death, but the mind governed by the Spirit is life and peace.

Romans 8:6

The biggest obstacle I have had to face in my journey for mental wellness is my emotions. Although this is a book aimed at mental health, I had to address the role emotions play in mental instability. I have learned that my emotions ruled me, sometimes (often) past the point of logic. With this understood, you can determine that if your emotional health is off, then almost certainly, your mental health can be affected negatively.

Biblical principles such as prayer and scripture will remind you of God's love and your worth and so much more, which all contribute to your emotional state. For years I applied biblical principle to what I wanted God to get rid of, but I wasn't applying it from a healthy state of mind or heart. I wanted God to fix me, but I didn't even understand how bad off I was emotionally and that my emotional trauma caused my mental breakdowns.

I was asking him to fix me, but I was still in the environment that triggered my emotional distress. How can he help me when

I am continuing to poison myself?

Once I removed myself from an unhealthy environment, I gradually realized that I was being ruled by my emotions. Emotions should be used as a guide to what is going on inside of us. Worry, fear, and anger can consume us if we let them. Every day, we must choose to believe God and trust his Word over how we feel and what we think.

Emotions are fleeting, but God's Word is forever. I had to learn this and practice choosing to believe God. The more I practiced, the more I noticed a change not only in my emotional awareness but in controlling emotional reactions. I had to remain aware of my thoughts and not allow negative thoughts to get comfortable in my mind—replacing every negative thought with a positive one. When worry starts to drown your mind, cloud your vision, and emotions begin to turn you away from God's peace, you are doubting what God has promised. You are also forgetting his command not to worry about anything, but to pray. We are only here for a moment in the flesh; much of what we worry about is nothing compared to the glory that will be revealed to us (1 Pet. 4:13). Battling severe and social anxiety disorders caused me to struggle with obsessive and compulsive thoughts that are like a revolving door in my mind. My worries and fears would become magnified and would consume me to a point of being mentally paralyzed.

The more I took the time to be still, pray, learn who I am, and learn what God says about me, the easier it was for me to realize I did not have to suffer by drowning myself in worrisome thoughts or replaying emotionally distressing scenarios. My problems didn't go away, but God became bigger than my problems. My power and authority as a daughter of God took precedence over my emotions. It took persistence, it took practice, and it took prayer for me to break free from the hold of mental weakness. You will see many references to my therapist; therapy was also a key to putting my emotions in their proper place — in my control.

Emotions can be strong, but God is stronger. God is everlasting and unchanging. Only by trying him and trusting him will you experience his promises in abundance. I challenge you as I have challenged myself to try God in his Word (apply his advice as laid out in the Bible). Try him instead of following your emotions first. Begin praying for guidance when you feel lost in or close to an anxiety attack or bout of depression. Praise God in spite of your circumstances, and worship through pain, confusion, hurt, and even fear. Make a decision to focus on God more than your emotions. Remember, what you feed will thrive, and what you starve will die and lose its hold on you.

Prayer

Father, right now, I lift you up and glorify your name. I acknowledge that you are above and more powerful than any emotion I feel at any moment. You are stronger than all of my circumstances. I welcome you into my heart, your rightful place, and ask you to transform me as I choose not to lean on my own understanding but to acknowledge you in all of my ways. Help me to run to you in scripture, prayer, and wise counsel when I am tempted to act irrationally. Cause me to remember to be still when thoughts and emotions flood my mind and heart. Help me to be aware of my emotional state and to control my responses to things that challenge me. Help me to remember you and your Word when I am emotionally weak. Help me to mature in my thoughts and be healed emotionally so that I can live and love from a healthy place. In the name of Jesus, I claim my emotional healing and maturity. I thank you that I can seek you and find you and trust your direction even when it is difficult. I give you praise now for my emotional and mental breakthrough. Amen.

Focus

Replace all negative thoughts with positive words and thoughts.

Focus your attention and energy on worship and God's Word whenever you feel overwhelmed or worried.

Explore hobbies and activities that can help you to express your emotions responsibly.

Talk to a therapist who can help you sort out your thoughts and emotions.

Scripture

"Trust in the LORD with all your heart and lean not on your own understanding; in all your ways submit to him, and he will make your paths straight" (Prov. 3:5–6).

"The heart is deceitful above all things and beyond cure. Who can understand it?" (Jer. 17:9).

"Those who trust in themselves are fools, but those who walk in wisdom are kept safe" (Prov. 28:26).

MAKE YOURSELF FEEL LIKE IT!

No discipline seems pleasant at the time, but painful. Later on, however, it produces a harvest of righteousness and peace for those who have been trained by it.

Hebrews 12:11

Remember God's gift to you of free will. But also remember your gift back to him is how you utilize that gift. God tells us to delight ourselves in him, in his Word, and all things pertaining to him. We know that we have a daily battle between what our flesh desires and what our spirit desires. This can be even more daunting for those who struggle with mental illnesses.

When depression creeps in and anxiety tries to take over, you will have to will yourself to get up, let alone pray or go to church. But you must do this. I have battled depression and anxiety for many years, so I understand exactly how heavy and hopeless depression can make you feel. When dealing with breaking habits of the flesh and taking on habits that strengthen your spirit, you will have to condition yourself to feel like it. Make yourself get up. Encourage yourself to do what your flesh is running from. There is no task too minuscule for God, but you must take that first step.

When you wallow in sadness, you invite more sadness and heaviness. Don't let self-pity take hold of you and cause you to remain isolated within yourself. Rest if you need to, but do not wallow. Rest is good for the mind, emotions, and body, but be careful not to entertain habits that feed depression. You reap what you sow, so sow what you want to reap. Joy for joy, peace for peace, love for love. I discovered that the more I focus on my negative feelings, the more I was depressed. But when I began to be proactive in my healing by seeking therapy and opening up about what I was dealing with, I grew out of habits that fed depression and healed in the areas that caused depression. I trusted and depended on God to help me through each task I set out to do—prayer, therapy, eating, or even going for a walk.

God is definitely with us in the dark times, but it is up to us to get up and move out of those dark places in ourselves. We must take a step and trust that God will walk beside us.

Sometimes, you will not know what to do at all. You will feel stuck and unsure. During these times, practice your faith walk. Do your best to follow God's Word and instructions. Walk out his principles the best you know how and trust that God will do the rest. He will never forsake you. He is with you always. No thoughts, emotions, or sicknesses will cause him to leave you. So, I encourage you to move forward every day. Allow God to groom you. Get the help you need. Seek deliverance, counseling, and guidance from a trusted source. Stay connected to God, and he will help you through it even when it feels like he might not be there.

Prayer

Father, I pray the Holy Spirit will push me to commune with you at all times. It is when I am heavy with emotions and fatigue that I need you most, so help me to push past my feelings and seek you. I pray that the Holy Spirit will flow through me and cause me to combat all emotions that are not from you and that are not good for me. Let your fire be ignited in me and cause a burning away of all distractions and excuses today. In Jesus's name, amen.

Focus

Discipline yourself to take action. Do it regardless of how you feel.

Allow God into your daily tasks and challenges. Recite scripture and simply pray for strength when you don't want to face the day.

Feed your spirit with scripture, worship, and sermons. Seek joy and peace over any dark feeling. Remember, *seek* is an action word.

Develop habits that will lead to a lifestyle of worship and being in God's presence. This is very important for the comfort and soothing you will need on the really tough days.

Scripture

"God is spirit, and his worshipers must worship in the Spirit and in truth" (John 4:24).

"Let the message of Christ dwell among you richly as you teach and admonish one another with all wisdom through psalms, hymns, and songs from the Spirit, singing to God with gratitude in your hearts" (Col. 3:16).

"Father, if you are willing, take this cup from me; yet not my will, but yours be done" (Luke 22:42).

"Jesus looked at them and said, 'With man this is impossible, but with God all things are possible'" (Matt. 19:26).

DON'T LET YOUR EMOTIONS RULE

When we let emotions rule our thoughts, we are not secure mentally. When emotions rule what you think of others and yourself, you are as fleeting as your emotions. Work to see everything as God sees. View situations from a larger perspective knowing God is in control. Let faith in God rule your thoughts so your mind can be transformed. Train your mind to overpower your emotions and guide your actions.

What I learned is that our emotions have a one-dimensional view of multifaceted situations. They cause us to see situations from a limited perspective that is not balanced with sound logic—this can be volatile. If your decisions are made solely based on emotions, this causes you to leave out your rational mind, the intentions and feelings of others, and the long-term effect of any actions you decide to take.

My life was changed when I decided to change what I let rule me, and it began with the renewing of my mind. Surrender your mind to God while receiving the mind of Christ. Your emotions are real and tangible, but your reality does not have to be ruled by those emotions.

Prayer

Father, thank you for your guidance and love. I acknowledge that I have a hard time with (list the areas you struggle with) ____________, ____________, and ____________. As I seek you in your Word, help me to apply your instruction to every situation I face. I desire to have peace of mind and understand the role my emotions play in that peace. Help me to use my emotions as a guide instead of the only determination of how I handle my trials. Provide me with tools I can use when I cannot get a handle on the way I feel. I look forward to healing emotionally with your help. I give you glory now for my emotional growth. In Jesus's name, amen.

Focus

What are some of your emotional triggers and/or emotional weak spots (family, friends, pet peeves, self, anger, sadness, etc.)?

What steps will you take today to overcome those weak spots?

Scripture

"Who has known the mind of the Lord so as to instruct him? But we have the mind of Christ" (1 Cor. 2:16).

"Above all else, guard your heart, for everything you do flows from it" (Prov. 4:23).

"You, however, are not in the realm of the flesh but are in the realm of the Spirit, if indeed the Spirit of God lives in you. And if anyone does not have the Spirit of Christ, they do not belong to Christ. But if Christ is in you, then even though your body is subject to death because of sin, the Spirit gives life because of righteousness. And if the Spirit of him who raised Jesus from the dead is living in you, he who raised Christ from the dead will also give life to your mortal bodies because of his Spirit who lives in you" (Rom. 8:9-11).

DECENCY AND ORDER

But everything should be done in a fitting and orderly way.

1 Corinthians 14:40

When you struggle with staying focused, disciplined, and organized, applying God's principle of order is key. The Word says there is a time for everything (Eccles. 3:1-8), and there are many events in our daily lives that should have a proper place and time.

It is important to operate with order so there is less room for the enemy to lead us astray. I have always been polarized with consistency and order. I was either extremely organized and consistent or extremely the opposite. Even my strong areas of organization and order were weaker when I was depressed and anxiety was at its worst. Anything could throw my routine off and cause me to fall behind on things like keeping my house or car clean, getting to work on time, and scheduling my time effectively. For someone like me, who thrives on order and organization, this can lead to a snowball effect.

While in the emotionally abusive relationship and mentally distressing environment, I was challenged daily in keeping order and organization in my life. I had to fight daily to keep things in order, and many times I failed. Everything felt like it was falling around me and I couldn't do anything about it. To cope, I would shut down or ignore the things I didn't have the energy to fix or that were out of my control. What I realized during this time was that I needed consistency and order, and lacking those things added to the stress that was already present. I hadn't realized how my structured upbringing and lifestyle prior to the dark period of my life had been beneficial for my psychological health and overall happiness.

I had to make a plan to get control of every area of my life in order to thrive in every area of my life.

I always desired stability but failed to achieve it, so I had to do my part for this to come to fruition. I needed to evaluate what was causing the instability. My abundant life depended on it. So, my plan was simple: one step at a time, be patient with myself and be persistent even when I lapsed in consistency. Every time I failed at keeping up with a meal plan, a workout plan, a prayer plan, a cleaning plan, or any other plan to bring order to my daily life, I would just pick up where I left off and even adjust to make sure my chances for success were increased.

Having a routine sets a standard for you to stay focused. A routine sets boundaries that keep confusion and distractions from impeding on your life. However, with order comes discipline.

If discipline is what is keeping you from your stability, ask God for help and do your best to stay the course. What has worked for me is writing down short-term goals that can be met in six months or less. Once I have these goals set, I write out weekly tasks that will contribute to those short-term goals. I have many things I would like to accomplish — we all do — but understanding the importance of starting small is key to making sure we stick to the tasks we set before us.

For example, if you want to pray more, instead of saying you will pray and meditate for an hour every morning at 4 a.m., start with two minutes of prayer and affirmations every morning when you wake up, and consider waking up ten or thirty minutes earlier if time isn't on your side. Stick with it and grow from there. You may find yourself praying more without having to consciously add time to your session.

Prayer

Father, I glorify and magnify your name. I hope to please you and apply your Word to every area of my life. Help me to organize my time and tasks and to be disciplined in keeping a schedule. Help me to be fervent and diligent in completing my daily tasks. I pray I will not succumb to confusion, stagnation, laziness, or any debilitating traits of depression. Also, help me not to condemn myself if I do not get it right every day, but help me to be consistent and dependable for myself and others. I thank you for your guidance and grace. In Jesus's name, amen.

Focus

Make a plan, make it plain, and walk it out.

Acknowledge your weaknesses and seek help in overcoming them.

Examine your life for things that disrupt your peace.

Scripture

"For God is not a God of disorder but of peace, as in all the congregations of the Lord's people" (1 Cor. 14:33).

"If anyone does not know how to manage his own family, how can he take care of God's church?" (1 Tim. 3:5).

OVER AND OVER AGAIN

Have I not commanded you? Be strong and courageous. Do not be afraid; do not be discouraged, for the LORD your God will be with you wherever you go.

Joshua 1:9

It is difficult to move forward when we focus on our shortcomings. We are our hardest critic, and if we aren't careful, we can think ourselves out of our progress. When trying to transform your life, setbacks are inevitable.

I am learning that the biggest mistake is dwelling on those shortcomings. Stop putting a limit on yourself because you didn't get it right or didn't do it perfectly. God forgives our shortcomings and knows we're going to have them, and he showed us grace because of it (we should still try our best to please God and answer the high calling he has for our life). Give yourself grace and be transformed by the wisdom gained through experience. Never be afraid to try again, and always believe that this time will be the time you get it right!

As I look back at where I was and how far I've come, I realize that with each trial and battle, I have progressed. The progress is not always noticeable right away. Sometimes it isn't recognized until weeks or months or even years later. The key for me was simply to keep trying, even when insecurities and doubt were present. After trying over and over again, I have gained wisdom, strength, endurance, and faith. Sometimes we focus so much on the negative that we fail to see our progress and God's love and presence through it all.

Prayer

Father God, thank you for your grace. Thank you for your love and patience with me on my journey through life. Help me to see the ways I limit myself and even you because of my own discouragement and lack of faith. Help me to remember what you think of me and say about me when I see myself as less than. Thank you for giving me access and equipping me with limitless power and potential through you. Amen.

Focus

Remain positive through all opposition and failures.

Practice speaking positive affirmations at your lowest points.

Recognize your successes and remember them in your prayers of thanks.

Scripture

"'For I know the plans I have for you,' declares the LORD, 'plans to prosper you and not to harm you, plans to give you hope and a future'" (Jer. 29:11).

"'But as for you, be strong and do not give up, for your work will be rewarded'" (2 Chron. 15:7).

KEEP PRESSING

I press on toward the goal to win the prize for which God has called me heavenward in Christ Jesus.

Philippians 3:14

When we seem to lose our way, haunting thoughts creep in. Guilt, condemnation, insignificance, alienation, despair, and other feelings can try to take over. God's Word is a perfect support and motivator to remind you that you are not alone. But reading scripture is only the first step. Believing and practicing what God says is what brings scripture to life in our lives. Hebrews 4:12 gives us an illustration of how God's Word works for those who read it: "For the word of God is alive and active. Sharper than any double-edged sword, it penetrates even to dividing soul and spirit, joints and marrow; it judges the thoughts and attitudes of the heart." To me this says that reading God's Word helps to get rid of what doesn't matter, cutting away what is keeping me from focusing on and pressing toward the calling God has on my life. This calling says I have hope and a future (Jer. 29:11) and an abundant life (John 10:10).

In some of my lowest, loneliest, and darkest moments, reading God's Word helped me to get back up, realize I am not alone, and see the light at the end of the tunnel. From those moments, I learned the value of pressing through the heaviness of depression and through the chaos of anxiety and even the pain of heartbreak.

No matter what you feel, nothing can separate you from the love of God or change what God says about you and the life he desires you to live.

Do not give up because you think you cannot "get it together." Remember that in our weakness, our Lord is strong. What matters is that you continue to press toward the mark of the high calling (Phil. 3:14), not giving in to sin and unhealthy mindsets but rising above them with persistence, practice, and prayer.

Prayer

Father, I lift you up and glorify your name. You are the lifter of my head, and I am grateful that I can do all things through you. Please help me to have hope when I want to give up and light whenever I am surrounded by dark thoughts and emotions. Show me how to be a beacon of light and hope to others around me as you are light and hope for me. Thank you for your Word and the guidance and strength I get when I read it. Help me to meditate on and remember your Word every day. In Jesus's name, amen.

Focus

Press toward the mark of the high calling.

Allow God to work on you. He is here to help.

Do not give up on God even when you can't hear or feel him, and do not give up on yourself.

Scriptures

"Have I not commanded you? Be strong and courageous. Do not be afraid; do not be discouraged, for the LORD your God will be with you wherever you go" (Josh. 1:9).

CHECK YOURSELF

Let us examine our ways and test them, and let us return to the LORD.

Lamentations 3:40

Stop! Sometimes the Holy Spirit will lead us to take a seat (or several). When things were going crazy around me and I did not understand why, I began to make it a habit to check myself. Even when I knew I was wronged, or even if there were circumstances outside of my control.

It is always good to see where you are spiritually, mentally, emotionally, and even physically. You cannot control much outside of your own actions. But you can control you. If you know and control your state of mind during times of distress, you can adjust and move forward with a positive mindset. As a believer, it is a good practice to bring these adjustments under the subjection of the Word of God. The Bible tells us more about what he plans for us. So in making adjustments, try to apply God's way and not your own (Prov. 3:5). Be honest with yourself and with God, and go to him with the changes you need to make. Then initiate change and allow God to transform you in that area. This is a tough one for me, as I can imagine it is for most.

For a while I allowed the chaos around me to rise above who I know I am in Christ. I had to take inventory of my thoughts and emotions. Things weren't going my way. I was uncomfortable and tired of the disappointments that I could not control. I made the decision to starve the parts of me that wanted to feed the distressing thoughts. I cried, I prayed, and I sat down and meditated on God's Word by reading and thinking of how I could apply his Word to my circumstances. In making this a routine, I was able to shift my focus and realign my thoughts.

This practice must be done continuously though. Yes, I am aware of those things I cannot control, but ultimately God is the one in control. So when I check myself, ultimately I have to decide to focus on what is out of my control or on *who* is in control. By focusing on who is in control, you will learn to trust God more and see your life from a lens of peace regardless of what is happening around you. Either way, God does not expect us to succeed without sometimes making mistakes. We must understand that no matter what struggles we face or imperfections we discover, God has always known they were there (Exod. 4:10-13). And better than that, he is not turning a blind eye to them but putting them to use for our good (Rom. 8:28). Matt. 14:29-31 can help you see the importance of keeping your focus on God versus worrying about what is going on around you.

> "Come," he said. Then Peter got down out of the
> boat, walked on the water and came toward Jesus.
> But when he saw the wind, he was afraid and,
> beginning to sink, cried out, "Lord, save me!"

> Immediately Jesus reached out his hand and caught him. "You of little faith," he said, "why did you doubt?"

Jesus did the "checking" for Peter by acknowledging Peter's lack of faith. In every storm we face, we ought to ask ourselves the same question that Jesus posed to Peter whenever we become doubtful: "why did you doubt?" Really, think about what causes you to doubt and compare those causes with who you have known God to be before and who he says he is in his word.

For years, I was having chronic anxiety attacks that seemed to come out of nowhere sometimes. It was very distressing and frustrating, and I would feel so alone and misunderstood because it felt like no one around me could really help me. An anxiety attack would be the storm, in this case, a feeling of chaos and terror that seems to have no end in sight. After doing some introspection (not during an actual anxiety attack), I was able to recognize that my environment and the way I viewed my environment were major factors in the anxiety I felt. My fears and worries were so deeply embedded in my mind that I would become "triggered" without even realizing it, which caused me to believe I was having these attacks for no reason, and if there was no reason, I was without hope of them ever stopping.

Once I was able to sit down, dig deep, and be honest about what was discovered, I was able to make strides and ultimately be relieved of chronic anxiety attacks. I practiced trusting God over worrying about my fears. It was like a mental trust fall, where I would imagine myself turning away from the worry of that moment and falling into the presence and promises of God. Every time my mind would try to tell me to worry about what was happening around me, I would tell myself to trust God by focusing my attention on God in prayer, reading his word, worshiping, and fellowshipping with other believers and positive friends and family. It is also important to note that this work wasn't during the anxiety attacks, but before and after. I realize that the anxiety attack was the result of mounting problems, and the removal of these attacks would be the result of addressing those problems. Even if I had to do it a dozen times.

The help I got from my therapist also helped me to recognize when my feelings and thoughts were rational and when they weren't—and the importance of replacing the irrational thoughts with rational ones.

Prayer

Father, I need your help! Lead me away from distractions, and help me to be aware of where my thoughts and emotions are taking me. If I get off course, I pray you redirect me and deliver me from destruction and distraction. Help me to put circumstances in perspective with your Word and the knowledge of who I am in you. Teach me how to adjust my life, my thoughts, and my words so that they line up with your precepts. I welcome you into my heart and mind to restore and revive, in Jesus's name, amen.

Focus

With each meal today, take time to assess your thoughts and feelings. Consider whether those thoughts and feelings are good or bad when compared to God's word. If they are bad, focus on ways you can realign yourself with a more positive mindset.

Scripture

"Examine yourselves to see whether you are in the faith; test yourselves. Do you not realize that Christ Jesus is in you — unless, of course, you fail the test?" (2 Cor. 13:5).

"Search me, God, and know my heart; test me and know my anxious thoughts. See if there is any offensive way in me and lead me in the way everlasting" (Ps. 139:23-24).

"Everyone ought to examine themselves before they eat of the bread and drink from the cup" (1 Cor. 11:28).

CHECK YOURSELF WORKSHEET

1. Check yourself, respect yourself. You do not deserve to be treated that way.

Think of the ways you allowed yourself to be disrespected or mistreated. Write about it. How did this affect your mental and emotional well-being? What part did you play?

2. Love yourself. Do things to remind yourself that you are worth fighting for.

Think of the areas in your life that you have neglected. Write about it and how you can change that today.

3. Encourage yourself. Remind yourself it's okay—you'll bounce back. You'll get through this.

Acknowledge your deepest regrets and biggest mistakes. Confess them. What have you learned from them?

4. Give yourself a break. Move on after realizing what you did wrong and how you can fix it.

Give yourself a pep talk and make an action plan that incorporates the lessons from these mistakes. Tell yourself a positive thing that counteracts every regret, mistake, and negative thought you have considered or written.

5. Remind yourself who you are. You are fearfully made. You are an overcomer!

Tell yourself that you are not your mistakes. Write a list of ten positive traits you see in yourself and write ten affirmations to support this view of yourself. Use the following scriptures as a guide and reminder of how God sees you:

"I praise you because I am fearfully and wonderfully made; your works are wonderful; I know that full well" (Ps. 139:14).

"You, dear children, are from God and have overcome them, because the one who is in you is greater than the one who is in the world" (1 John 4:4).

"For this is what the LORD Almighty says: 'After the Glorious One has sent me against the nations that have plundered you — for whoever touches you touches the apple of his eye'" (Zech. 2:8).

# GOD WILL NOT ABANDON YOU

Say to those with fearful hearts, 'Be strong, do not fear;
your God will come, he will come with vengeance; with
divine retribution he will come to save you.'

Isaiah 35:4

For those who have suffered depression to any degree, I am sure you can agree that it is one of the loneliest things you have experienced. Along with fear and paranoia, which can also be experienced under the umbrella of PTSD and anxiety disorder, depression can cause one to feel alone regardless of who is around them. I have felt that way many times. I am grateful that I was able to discover peace and hope in the promises of God even when my condition says I am prone to feel hopeless and unsettled. But to experience peace and hope, I had to try God.

Psalms 34:8 tells us to "taste and see that the LORD is good," and this tells me that the only way to get the goodness of God is to follow the advice he has given in his word. Psalms 34:8 finishes with "blessed is the one who takes refuge in him." What I have learned is that even when I feel alone, if I take refuge in God, I will never truly be alone. I only came to this conclusion after making the decision to accept that God has never left me, and he never will.

It took one decision on a dark, lonely night to trust God over the reality of my emotions and thoughts. That one decision to believe that God was not far off—even though it felt like he was—led to more decisions of faith (it is not a one-time thing). This caused me to be bolder and more hopeful than ever before as my faith grew.

God came through to me in many ways: a phone call from a friend, a prayer or scripture sent by text because I was on someone's mind, a hug from a loved one, a healing conversation, or even a confirming sermon. Sometimes God would come and just allow me to feel joy, peace, and comfort in his presence. These moments would happen every day and would be so timely that I could not deny that God was showing me he was close and that he was taking care of me. He gave me exactly what I needed when I allowed him with my faith. Hebrews 11:6 explains that "without faith it is impossible to please Him" and that "he who comes to God must believe that He is and that He is a rewarder of those who seek Him."

It is true that God will never leave you or forsake you, but if you want to see him and experience him in a life-changing way, try faith. This is something that no one can do for you—you must try it on your own. But from experience I can testify that the more I believed, the more my faith grew. Each time I decided to trust God, God blessed me. So now when trials come, if I don't see or feel anyone around me, I remind myself that God is close and he is pulling me through whatever comes my way.

Prayer

Father God, thank you for your saving grace and your mercy. Sometimes it is hard to have hope, but I desire for my faith in you to grow. Help me to please you with my faith and try your goodness according to your promises. As I learn to take refuge in you, bless me with your peace and joy. Help me to open up to you and allow you to heal the hurting parts of my soul. Give me the courage to wait for you to move on my behalf, and wisdom so I may know when I need to act for myself. In Jesus's name, amen.

Focus

Memorize Psalms 91.
Trust that God is a deliverer.

Scripture

"I sought the LORD, and he answered me; he delivered me from all my fears" (Ps. 34:4).

NO BONDAGE

So if the Son sets you free, you will be free indeed.

John 8:36

God tells us that for every temptation we experience, he provides an escape (1 Cor. 10:13). As believers in Christ Jesus, we know that God has set us all free from mental, emotional, physical, and spiritual bondage. This does not mean that nothing displeasing will ever happen to us. It means that we are free from the weight of those displeasing things. We have the promise of salvation from death. We have a promise that nothing can overpower us or prevail against us. But so many times we are tempted to doubt that we are indeed free as God says we are. Accepting the truth of our freedom in Christ can be more challenging if depression, anxiety, and other mental illnesses have weighed us down. But the good thing is that God's promise of freedom is for all. He has a strategy of escape made just for you. Knowing that God never leaves us and is a constant guide, I believe that as we get to know his voice, he can walk us through the obstacles of our freedom and straight to the liberty of his presence.

Bondage occurs because we allow the enemy's lies to

ensnare us and discourage us. Remember, who the Son sets free is free indeed (John 8:36). Do you believe this? I was easily persuaded to live as if I were not free. I began to understand that my freedom was already granted, but my actions, my words, and my thoughts would be what walked me out of the open prison doors. I had to change my speech from "I don't think I can do this" to "I can do all things through Christ." Instead of just crying, I began to encourage and affirm myself through scripture. *God is the lifter of your head, Danielle. No weapon formed against you can prosper, Danielle. Peace is your portion, Danielle.* I realized my freedom was not only in praying for the gates to be opened, but my freedom was also in me deciding that I wanted to be free and that I would walk through the gates. But first I had to believe that I was free in Christ.

Prayer

Father, I thank you for setting me free. Help me to explore, learn, and maintain my freedom in you. Help me to see the habits I practice that don't represent my freedom. Help me to seek you, ask of you, and knock on your door when my past sins and problems try to imprison me again. I pray I will have the diligence to maintain my freedom and follow in the footsteps of Jesus. Help me to recognize the lies and traps of the enemy when he tries to convince me I am not free indeed. I pray I can be bold in my freedom and glorify your name with my entire life. In Jesus's name, amen.

Focus

Exercise your freedom by expressing your emotions and thoughts with others you can trust.

Monitor your actions and words today. Do they represent bondage or freedom?

Scripture

"It is for freedom that Christ has set us free. Stand firm, then, and do not let yourselves be burdened again by a yoke of slavery" (Gal. 5:1).

THE LORD IS CHEERING YOU ON

. . . He will take great delight in you; in his love he will no longer rebuke you, but will rejoice over you with singing.

Zephaniah 3:17

God is rooting for you! He calls you victorious because you are his. He sees you and all that have disappointed and hurt you. He sees all your shortcomings, and he still longs for you. He still cheers you on and is your number one supporter. You are the apple of his eye, his fearfully and wonderfully made creation. He desires for you to know these things. He is the lifter of your head, and he calls you royalty. He sees everything about you and still believes in you!

I know this because after all that I have suffered through mentally, he helped me, teaching me and guiding me even when I resisted. He has been patient with me as any loving father would.

As soon as I recognized I was off track, God stepped right back in as if nothing happened and nudged me along, encouraging me all the way. Every time I had a bad thought, I would be reminded of a scripture that combatted it. God has a word of encouragement for every obstacle I will ever face. I know he does this with all his children, although many times he makes me feel like I am all he sees. I know he feels this same deep love and desire for you too. So if you haven't realized already, please believe it today. God is cheering you on.

Even when it doesn't feel this way, be encouraged by the promises in his word. He knows what he created in you and what you have on the inside that needs to be released into the world. Let God encourage you, and in turn, encourage someone else. The world needs you, and God calls us all to love and encourage each other as a parent would want for brothers and sisters. He isn't just cheering you on for you. He is cheering you on because someone will be at the finish line waiting for your advice, encouragement, and example. And then you can help them hear God's cheering too.

So when you are feeling discouraged, keep God's word close. When your head is down, read his promises and let his word uplift you. There have been countless days when I went from down in the dumps to on top of the world, and all I did in those moments was spend time with God. I sang songs of praise and thanks, I prayed, and I read the lessons, pep talks, and love letters he provided in the Bible. God didn't send his instructions to us because he doesn't think we can do what he has called us to do—he gave us instructions in great detail because he knows we can.

Prayer

Father, thank you for your never-ending love and support. Help me to recognize your encouragement when I feel stuck and alone. Help me to push past insecurities and believe in myself as much as you believe in me. I want to be the best me I can be, and I welcome you in my life to help me reach my optimum potential. May your word penetrate my mind and fill my heart so that I will remain encouraged in Christ Jesus. Amen.

Focus

Believe in yourself. Believe that God is cheering you on and that he made you for a special purpose.

Be encouraged. I love to listen to a nice, upbeat praise song when I feel a case of the blues trying to kick in.

Scripture

"For your ways are in full view of the LORD, and he examines all your paths" (Prov. 5:21).

"But you are a chosen people, a royal priesthood, a holy nation, God's special possession, that you may declare the praises of him who called you out of darkness into his wonderful light" (1 Pet. 2:9).

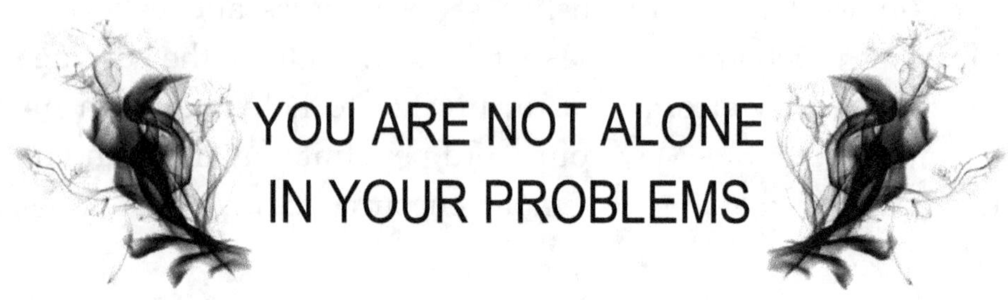

YOU ARE NOT ALONE IN YOUR PROBLEMS

When I saw him, I fell at his feet as though dead. Then he placed his right hand on me and said: 'Do not be afraid. I am the First and the Last.'

Revelation 1:17

I am not the first to experience what I am dealing with, even though sometimes I feel like I am the only one. But I won't be the last to feel alone in the fiery trials of life. The truth is *you* aren't the first in your own struggles and failures, and you won't be the last either. But this means you're not alone. Part of my motivation to overcome my struggles with mental illness was the thought of being able to tell someone else struggling with their mental health how I did it. As a believer who desires to make the world a better place, it is our duty to turn back and help those who are dealing with what we are dealing with.

Mental health bears a stigma, and this stigma is evident in a variety of ways across many demographics. From not being discussed or expressed, to over-medicating or even labeling someone with mental health issues as an attention-seeker, it is easy in this day and age to feel alone and helpless if they struggle psychologically. There is not a cookie-cutter solution for every person whose reality is that of mental illness. More resources are needed for treatment, support groups, and discussions to allow for more education and understanding. In many churches (not all) some may try only to pray for what needs to be brought to the attention of a therapist, counselor, or medical doctor. It is also important to make sure the conversation about mental health not only continues but grows and gains facets that can extend to demographics that may not have had mental health support they needed in the past.

Jesus explains that he is "the light of the world" and that "whoever follows [him] will never walk in darkness" (John 8:12). What makes this even better is that you and I are commanded to be "a light for the Gentiles that [we] may bring salvation to the ends of the earth" (Acts 13:47). Often when I think of light, I think of exposure, knowledge, and truth. Darkness, of course, would be the opposite: concealment, ignorance, and lies.

With mental health being something that is dark, often undetected because of shame and/or ignorance, I believe it is very important to shine a light on this crisis. We can shine a light by simply saying something to someone about what we are going through, what we are doing about it, and what we believe can help us and others who are suffering with us. Matthew 5:15-16 gives a great example of shining our light (talents, services, information) before others "that they may see your good deeds and glorify your Father in heaven." You may not feel like you are in a place to help anyone now by sharing your current situation. But you would be surprised by who you can bless just by talking about what you have been dealing with. You may also end up receiving help in return for being transparent.

People have experienced depression, anxiety, and suicidal thoughts and have overcome them. There are counselors and therapists who have studied and specialized in mental health. There are support groups, churches, ministries, your own friends, family, and mental health hotlines. All of these resources can be utilized for your healing. I personally depended on friends, my church family, mentors, my therapist, and my medical doctor. Ultimately, when my day was over and I was alone, I brought everything back to God in thanks, because without his provision, I wouldn't have so many open lines of support. I was and continue to be thankful that he provided so many resources for me to prosper. I am thankful that I tapped into the Light of the World and, in turn, am enabled to be a beacon of light for others.

I encourage you to plug directly into the true healer, the redeemer, our Father who cares for us and knows us more than any person ever will.

Have solace in knowing that God, the alpha and omega, is with you and has made it so that everything you need to win the battles you face is at your disposal.

Prayer

Father God, thank you for all you are doing in my life — even the things I do not understand. I pray that my testimony will glorify you and be a testament to your love for me. Help me to see you in every area of my life as you walk with me through the valleys and the fields. I welcome you to pour into my life, heal my heart, and restore my soul. Bless me, and help me to be a blessing today. Lead me out of timidity and fear. Lead me into boldness and courage. Help me to turn the negatives in my life into a positive for someone else. Endow me to be a true and right representative of you. I give you all glory, honor, and praise, in Jesus's name, amen.

Focus

Pray for and encourage others.

Consider sharing your struggles or testimony with someone.

Look into seeking therapy if you haven't already.

Scripture

"Be alert and of sober mind. Your enemy the devil prowls around like a roaring lion looking for someone to devour. Resist him, standing firm in the faith, because you know that the family of believers throughout the world is undergoing the same kind of sufferings" (1 Pet. 5:8-9).

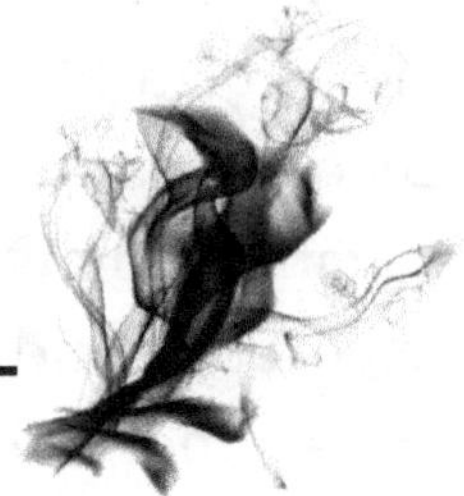

WHOLE. FREE. FEARLESS. FAITHFUL

And the God of all grace, who called you to his eternal glory in Christ, after you have suffered a little while, will himself restore you and make you strong, firm, and steadfast.

1 Peter 5:10

In a conversation with God, I asked him to help me through this valley I am currently in. He responded with, "I am already helping you through. Now tell me what you want." Now I understand he wanted me to be specific and to shift my focus from the hardship to my heart's desires and goals. As I began talking, all I said boiled down to wanting to be whole, free, fearless, and still faithful.

I am in a season of brokenness and uncertainty that I know will require God to heal and restore me. I asked him to restore me and let me stay restored. I was looking for the peace that comes with being made whole. I also asked to be free. Free from emotions that arrested me and hindered me. Free from double-mindedness and doubt. Free from the heaviness and heartache I had been experiencing. Next, I asked him for fearlessness so that worry wouldn't be able to plague my heart and mind.

Worrying about our worst fears coming true won't always keep them from happening. Remember, God has not given us the spirit of fear, but of power, love, and a sound mind (2 Tim. 1:7). Also, perfect love cast out fear (1 John 4:18). So, focus on the power you have as a child of God to conquer even your emotions and fears, remembering that all things work together for your good (Rom. 8:28).

I thought of how Eve was already whole when God created her, yet the enemy still tricked her. So I prayed that I could remain faithful in my dark season even though the enemy tried to trick me with lies, saying I wouldn't get through my hardships.

And when God completes the good work he began in me and makes me whole, free, and fearless, I prayed I wouldn't forget who did it and would remain faithful in my walk and witness and testimony.

I know my best life will always be with God in it, and I pray I cling to him when I am whole, free, and fearless by continuing to seek him and serve him.

Every advancement in my growth, big or small, I can attribute to God. I have learned to carefully consider exactly how God orchestrated each success I have experienced to ensure I remember that he is the one who made everything possible. By doing this, I am able to keep all my victories and lessons learned in proper perspective and continue to seek help from God as I continue to glorify him for those victories and lessons. God is intricately weaved into all the tools I use to overcome the struggles that I face due to mental illness. He helped me to build a lifestyle that supports a healthy mind. It would be dangerous for me to forget God and all that he has helped me with. Forgetting to keep God at the center of this new lifestyle can easily cause me to get off track.

The key is to continually welcome God in your life via prayer, worship, and Bible study. Invite him into every aspect of your life, and he will help you maintain all that you have prayed and worked so hard for.

Prayer

Father, thank you for your never-ending and unfailing love. Thank you for enduring with me and fighting for me in every situation that rises against me. I realize I am not perfect and in fact broken, and I need you to fix me. Help me to gain my wholeness and healing from you and no other. Grant me access to all you have placed inside of me, and cause me to be bold and fearless because of who I am in you. Help me to dig deep when I want to give up. I pray I never forget where I have been delivered from and that your power delivered me. May my life be a light that shines for your glory! In Jesus's name, amen.

Focus

Remain in the shadow of God. Do not neglect prayer, worship, and Bible study just because things are going how you want them to.

Scripture

"Come to me, all you who are weary and burdened, and I will give you rest. Take my yoke upon you and learn from me, for I am gentle and humble in heart, and you will find rest for your souls" (Matt. 11:28-29).

"For the Spirit God gave us does not make us timid, but gives us power, love, and self-discipline" (2 Tim. 1:7).

"Therefore, my dear friends, as you have always obeyed — not only in my presence, but now much more in my absence — continue to work out your salvation with fear and trembling, for it is God who works in you to will and to act in order to fulfill his good purpose" (Phil. 2:12-13).

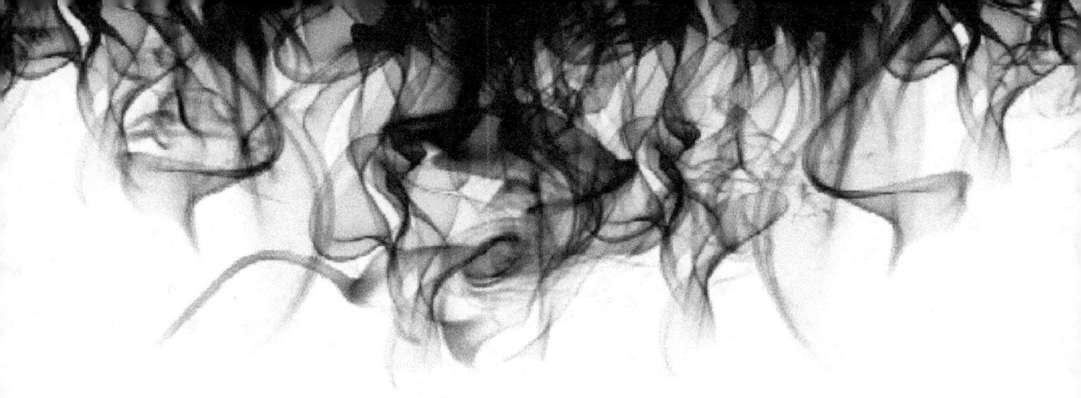

AFFIRMATIONS

WALKING INTO YOUR POWER
SPEAK INTO YOUR LIFE AND SELF

Death and life are in the power of the tongue, and those who love it will eat its fruits.

Proverbs 18:21

AFFIRMATIONS

Then the LORD *replied: 'Write down the revelation and make it plain on tablets so that a herald may run with it.'*

Habakkuk 2:2

This segment is a guide that highlights the importance of knowing and using the power of your spoken word. Affirmations are used by many people of different backgrounds and religious beliefs. I began using affirmations and can testify that this simple practice has had a major effect on the way I feel about myself and what I encounter. We have creative power with our words, just like our Father in heaven. We can create and change our realities by speaking it into existence with affirmations and prayer.

I also listed the different names of God because it helped me grasp how many ways God is God. Sometimes people can limit God and all he can do. Learning the meanings of the different names he has as listed in the Bible (in the original text before all his names were translated to simply *God*) helped me to learn that there is nothing too big for him to help me with. Next, I recognize that as his children made in his image, knowing who he is, is key to us knowing exactly who we are. Battling with mental illness can make you feel distant from anything that describes you as a child of God. Learning and using these names in prayer and affirmation helps me to connect to all of God, so I keep his many names at the forefront of my mind when I am dealing with a hard time.

AFFIRM WHO YOU BELONG TO

El Shaddai: my God is God almighty.
No one is greater than my God

Adonai: my Lord
my ruler, my maker, and my keeper

Elohim: my God is strong and is the creator of all things
the world is in his hands
he controls all things
he gives and he takes away
he destroys and he builds up

Jehovah Rapha: my healer and restorer

Jehovah Jireh: my God is my provider

Jehovah Nissi: my God is my banner
He sets the example for mankind
He speaks to us and for us

Jehovah Shalom: my God is my peace

Jehovah Raah: my God is my shepherd. He leads my way

Jehovah Tsidkenu: my God is my righteousness

Jehovah Shammah: my God is my light and is always around

Abba: my Father in heaven

AFFIRM WHO GOD IS

You are my deliverer.
You are my healer.
You are the lifter of my head.
You are love.
You are my strong tower I run to and am safe.
You vindicate me.
You are my comforter.
You are my peace.
You are my teacher.
You are Alpha and Omega.
You are the lion of Judah and you protect me.
You are my Abba.
You are high and lifted up.
You are the keeper of my gates.
You are omnipotent.
You are omnipresent.
You are the lily in the valley.
You are my hope, my strength, and my shield.
You are Jehovah Jireh.
Your name is matchless.
You are the great I Am.
You are my rock and my fortress.
You are my strength.
Your grace and mercy carry me.

AFFIRM WHO YOU ARE

I am a child of the most high God.

I am fearfully and wonderfully made.

I am a royal priest.

I am the apple of God's eye.

I am equipped to war and to battle.

I am called to Christ.

No weapon formed against me shall prosper.

I am victorious through Christ Jesus.

I can do all things through Christ who strengthens me.

I am the head and not the tail.

I am blessed and not cursed.

I am above and not beneath.

I am prosperous.

I am confident.

I have a sound mind.

I am fearless.

I am loved.

I am redeemed.

I am confident.

I am beautiful.

I am made in God's image.

I am here on purpose.

BE BLESSED BY THE FRUIT OF YOUR LIPS

I shall decree a thing and it will come to pass.

I am blessed coming in and blessed going out.

I prosper as my soul prospers.

I have power love and a sound mind.

My family is blessed.

My marriage is blessed and not cursed.

I am blessed and not cursed.

My husband is blessed and not cursed.

Every negative word spoken against me is canceled and destroyed.

I am fruitful and will multiply.

My finances are blessed.

My children are blessed.

My charity is blessed.

My ministry is blessed.

My natural and supernatural vision is blessed.

I have power and authority to trample on snakes and scorpions.

I am fearfully and wonderfully made.

I am seated in heavenly places.

I am blessed to be a blessing.

My faith increases daily.

I will decree and see miracles signs and wonders from heaven.

I have the joy of the Lord.

Nothing can stop me.

I am victorious.
The works of my hands are blessed.
I am endorsed by God.
I am an overcomer.
I am redeemed through Christ Jesus.
I am renewed in Christ.
I am above and not beneath.
I can do all things through Christ who strengthens me.
I am free from all bondage and live in freedom.
I am free from depression and live in joy.
I am free from anxiety and live in peace.
I am free from confusion and live in clarity.
I am free from darkness and live in God's light.
I am free from lies and live in the truth.
I am free from sickness and live in health.
I am free as the Lord renews my strength.
I am free as the Lord renews my hope.
I am free as the Lord renews my peace.
I am free as the Lord renews my mind.
I am free as the Lord restores my soul.

WRITE YOUR OWN AFFIRMATIONS

A HEART-TO-HEART WITH GOD

From your heart to his. Leaving no stone unturned, spill your heart to God.

FINAL THOUGHTS

We made it! We made it further than yesterday and came out better than we were before. I can honestly say that I have grown and elevated since I began writing this journal. On some of my toughest days when I didn't want to go on, I pushed to share my story because I believed that God has a purpose in all my pain.

This journal is a stepping-stone. I learned that being stagnant in any negative emotion or headspace will cause self-destruction. Get all you need from this journal, your current trial, the process, clinical therapy, and spiritual counseling. Do all of this with the ultimate goal being to be free, move forward, and be renewed. It is a process. But trust God and trust that the process is all part of the plan. Look forward optimistically with hope. Believe and receive your healing.

With love,
Danielle

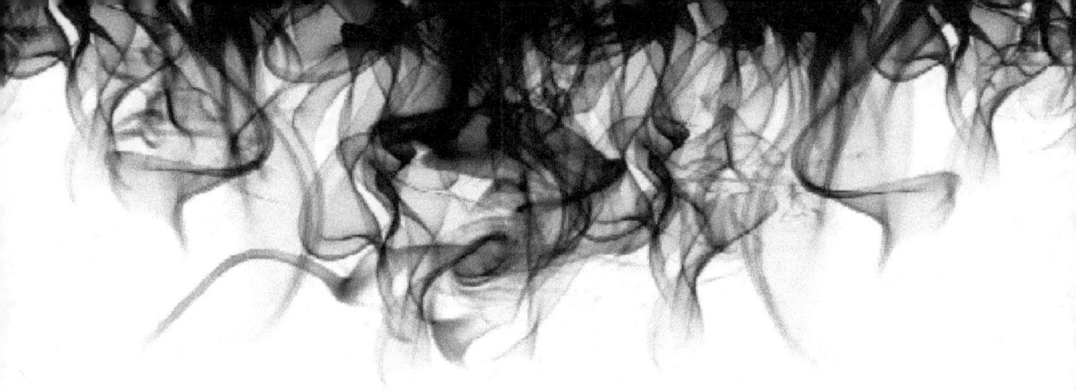

ABOUT THE AUTHOR

Danielle Presume is a Minister in Training at Temple of Faith Ministries located in Augusta, Georgia. She is a native of Miami, Florida where she began her journey in ministry as a Liturgical Dance Minister. In recent years she has answered the call as a Prophetic Intercessor and believes strongly in the power of prayer.

Danielle hopes to glorify God, inspire and change lives with her testimony by using her gifts and passions of writing and creative arts. Although *ANEW* is her first book, Danielle believes this is only the beginning and is excited to see what God has in store for her.